Katherine Ingmire

Living Pictures in the Church of the Holy Communion

and other thoughts in verse

Katherine Ingmire

Living Pictures in the Church of the Holy Communion
and other thoughts in verse

ISBN/EAN: 9783337286644

Printed in Europe, USA, Canada, Australia, Japan

Cover: Foto ©Lupo / pixelio.de

More available books at **www.hansebooks.com**

IN THE

Church of the Holy Communion,

AND

OTHER THOUGHTS IN VERSE.

BY

KATHARINE INGMIRE.

NEW YORK:
ANSON D. F. RANDOLPH & COMPANY,
900 BROADWAY, COR. 20th ST.

COPYRIGHT, 1878, BY
ANSON D. F. RANDOLPH & COMPANY.

"*In a good work our hopes should be high in the beginning, however we may fall short in the end. When Christ is the sure foundation-stone, elect and precious, we may piously trust that the temple of living stones may arise, animated by His Spirit, adorned by His grace, bound together by His love, and everywhere inscribed, Holiness to the Lord.*"

[*Dr. Muhlenberg's address at the laying of the corner-stone of the Church of the Holy Communion, New York, July* 24, 1844.]

Preface.

COMING to the Church of the Holy Communion thirty years after the words I have quoted were spoken by its first pastor, and carefully observing its work, I soon felt that the hopes must have been high indeed in the beginning that had not been already more than realized. On expressing my feelings in "Dreamland Church in Stone," I found I had only echoed the thoughts of hundreds, many of whom thanked me so warmly for that expression, and still ask for copies of it, that I have been tempted to send forth this volume (in aid of one of the many charities of the church), which I affectionately inscribe to the "dear, familiar friends" who now gather around me, and make me feel that I can no longer say with truth that I am a "lone, strange worshipper."

K. I.

Dreamland Church in Stone.

THOUGHTS ON THE CHURCH OF THE HOLY COMMUNION, NEW YORK.

"This shall be my rest forever; here will I dwell, for I have a delight therein."

A DREAMLAND Church once stood for me
   Within a charming book;
I never thought on church so fair
   With earthly eyes to look;
But when the last awaking came,
   And death's long sleep was o'er,
I hoped a fairer still to see
   Upon the eternal shore.

A stranger in the city, I
   Set out to find a home,
And wandered till I heard a bell
   That said so plainly, "Come,"

I could but choose to follow on,
    Drawn by a sound so sweet,
And thank the Lord, who to this place
    First led my weary feet.

For rest, and sweetest rest I found
    Within the dear church-wall
Where Mammon is exalted not,
    Where God is all in all.
Where praises flow as freely as
    The blessings God doth give;
Where Christ's own poor are feasted, and
    The poor in spirit live.

Where kindly deeds show forth the thanks
    The loving lips express;
Where alms "lend wings to prayer," and make
    A church that God doth bless.
Where I, an unknown worshipper
    Within the holy place,
Have sweet communion found, though not
    One dear, familiar face.

The loved and lost seem very near,
   The Saviour nearer still;
The Comforter comes down to me
   And shows the Father's will,
And with the unknown choir around
   I join the choir above,
And "Holy, Holy, Holy," sing,
   And taste the feast of love.

Now, next the church where I was born
   God's child and heir to be,
That gave through all my early years
   Her tender care to me,
I love the dear and precious church
   I found in sorrow's day,
That seemed to hold a wondrous power
   To charm my grief away.

And I—a lone, strange worshipper—
   When called afar to roam,
Leave not without a saddened heart
   The place I call my home,

For I have found that Dreamland Church
  Stands not alone in song;
That all the beauty church doth need
  Doth to this church belong.

God's favor rest upon their heads
  Who laid the glorious plan,
And built a Dreamland Church in stone
  To bless their fellow-man.
And may the bell for aye ring out
  That says so sweetly, "Come,"
And many seekers, through all time,
  Find here their Father's home.

A Thought in Church.

Among the joys of heaven
  The least may not be this;
The memory of holy hours
  That came so near its bliss.

Living Pictures

IN THE

CHURCH OF THE HOLY COMMUNION.

As in the interior of the dome of St. Peter's at Rome, stones of fair color present to the eye pictures of beauty, so do the "lively stones" in the Lord's house present pictures very pleasant, and never to be forgotten.

Morning.

THE CHILDREN'S BENCH.

"Out of the mouths of babes and sucklings Thou hast perfected praise."

    SITTING where the morning sun
      Is brightened by its fall
    Through the gay-tinted window
      High in the church's wall,

I see a row of maidens;
   Such little maidens they!
But none too young to listen,
   Or creed and prayer to say.

I often look with pleasure
   On some bright, happy face
That the canvas of Angelico
   Or Raphael might grace.

You would think they understood
   Every word the preacher said,
From the steady, earnest gaze,
   And the posé of the head.

And I think they understand;
   I'll tell the reason why.
I only know one rule to judge
   Both men and children by,

So I think they understand
   When they practice what they hear,

And that they do sometimes
  To me is very clear.

For deeds of thoughtful kindness
  I have known these children do,
And acts of self-denial
  I have seen them practice too.

I once overheard them say,
  " They loved their pastor so,"
And when asked the reason, said,
  " He's so good to us, you know."

Thus I see that love and pity
  And gratitude have found
A lodgment in their tender hearts
  Like seeds in fertile ground.

And I pray these little maidens
  May daily grow in grace,
And practice holy preaching
  Till they see the Saviour's face.

That the faithful pastor's crown
  As the stars of heaven may shine,
When God shall own his work, and say,
  " Thy children all are Mine."

Noonday.

THE LORD'S SUPPER.

"As oft as ye eat this bread, and drink this cup, ye do show the Lord's death till He come."

"He that eateth my flesh, and drinketh my blood, dwelleth in me and I in him."

SOMEWHERE in my travels a picture I've seen
   Of Luke, the beloved, in a trance;
His feet touch the earth, but a vision above
   Has caught and made captive his glance.

The clouds have rolled back, as the waves of the sea
   Once rolled at the prophet's command,
And through the bright pathway that opens beyond
   Comes a glimpse of the promisèd land;

And just at the entrance, the mother so meek,
   Whom all generations call blest,

Is standing and folding with tenderest care
  The holy Christ-child to her breast.

And while the Apostle is gazing, intent,
  The angels have come to his aid;
The colors, so rare, to the finest are ground,
  In wonderful order are laid.

His fingers are moved by the Spirit, unseen,
  In reply to his earnest prayer,
That the vision now glowing in beauty above
  May live on the canvas as fair.

   .   .   .   .

The sun from the zenith is pouring
  Its glory through each pictured pane,
And chasing the shades from each corner
  And nook of the holy fane.

The sun never shineth at noontide
  In this place, on the Lord's own day,
That shines not on loving disciples
  Assembled to praise and pray,

And partake of the holy emblems
   Of Christ's precious body and blood,
That give strength to resist the evil,
   And grace to follow the good.

The worshippers lowly are kneeling
   As the words of the prayer are said,
That shall make a heavenly feast for them
   Of the common wine and bread.

And as with the rest I am kneeling
   A vision seems coming to me;
Oh, would that the Spirit would aid me
   To paint the picture I see.

'Tis not of the child, and the mother
   With her exquisite, saintly grace,
But of One in the strength of manhood
   With worn and agonized face.

The sins of the world are upon Him,
   And now in the fierce noonday blaze

He is hung, and the surging rabble
  All mock and jest as they gaze.

The arms outstretched on the cruel cross
  Were ever extended to bless;
The feet now pierced were swift to go
  At the cry and call of distress.

But hushed are the people's hosannas,
  For envy and malice bear sway,
And fierce are the foes that stand nearest,
  And timid the friends far away.

The vision is closing in blackness;
  The sun its bright face hath withdrawn,
Refusing to shine on the anguish,
  The body so bleeding and torn.

But a voice seems to say from the darkness,
  "My body was broken for thee;
Forget not My dying commandment—
  Do this in remembrance of Me."

My thoughts come again to the present, ——
  And I gaze at the throng awhile
That is passing with softened footfall
  To the altar, down the aisle.

Both the young and the old are going;
  The old must have grace to die;
The young need much strength for the battles
  With sin that before them lie.

And the strong and the weak are going;
  The weak of much patience have need,
And the strong need the consecration
  Of love for their every deed.

The weary and heavily laden
  Are going that they may find rest;
The gay and light-hearted are going,
  For there they may be more blest.

And I know, dearest Lord, Thou art there;
  Thou hast promised to meet Thine own;

To come to hearts that forget Thee not,
  And in breaking of bread be known.

And I pray the lives of Thy children
  May reflect the beauty of Thine,
As on Saint Luke's canvas the picture
  Of the heavenly vision gave sign.

That life's work, by the aid of the Spirit,
  May wear a far holier grace
Because, through the way Thou hast opened,
  By faith we have seen Thy face.

Evening.

THE AGED WOMEN'S REST.

"Abide with us, for the day is far spent and the night is at hand."

THE dear Lord's day is ending;
　　The sun, far on its way,
Is passing through the western gate
　　To crown the western day.

And gray the shades are falling,
　　Where fell such glorious light
It seemed as if some rays from Christ
　　Were lent to make it bright,

To give His waiting children
　　A foretaste of that day
When in the heavenly temple
　　He shall give light alway.

Now as the shades grow darker
  I turn mine-eyes to where
The aged ones together meet
  For evening praise and prayer.

I know not by what ways they came
  To find this earthly rest;
I only know, that having found,
  They surely must be blest.

For memory lends her aid to read
  The look that I see there;
That look of saintly, calm repose
  None but the old can wear.

A look that ever seems to say,
  "The day is well-nigh done;
The shades of night are coming fast,
  But victory is won.

"The fight was long and steady,
  The soldiers sorely tried,

But in His strength they conquer
  Who serve the Crucified."

As with folded hands they wait,
  They scan the battle-field,
And praise the name of Him who made
  The strongest foeman yield.

On wrinkled brow and bending form,
  On failing ear and eye,
On heads of white and heads of gray
  The growing shadows lie,

That tell of night and darkness
  And the long, quiet rest;
The flesh in dreamless slumber,
  The soul among the blest.

Life's shadows lie behind them,
  Death's shadow lies before,
But only through its darkness
  They reach the shining door

That opens to receive them
   When shadows flee away,
And the King in all His beauty
   Is seen in perfect day.

Lullaby.

WRITTEN FOR THE CHILDREN IN THE BABIES'
SHELTER, IN CHARGE OF THE SISTERS
OF THE HOLY COMMUNION.

Air—"Adeste Fideles."

"Blessed are the pure in heart, for they shall see God."

SLEEP, baby, sleep, for thy Saviour is near;
With Him for a watcher thou needest not fear;
The tenderest babe in His love hath a part,
He keepeth the weakest the nearest His heart.
  His arm doth uphold them,
  His love doth enfold them,
Then sleep, baby, sleep, for thy Saviour is near.

Sleep, baby, sleep, for thy Saviour is near;
No father or mother can hold thee so dear;
Since for Him the innocents suffered and died,
He draweth young children all close to His side.

  His arm doth uphold them,
  His love doth enfold them,
Then sleep, baby, sleep, for thy Saviour is near.

Sleep, baby, sleep, for thy Saviour is near,
And sweet are His words as they fall on the ear,
" Forbid not the children to come unto Me,
For only the child-like My kingdom shall see."
  My arm shall uphold them,
  My love shall enfold them,
Then sleep, baby, sleep, for thy Saviour is near.

Sleep, baby, sleep, for thy Saviour is near;
Oh, serve Him forever, my baby, so dear.
Keep always as guileless as now in thy heart,
If thou from thy Saviour wouldst never depart.
  His arm shall uphold thee,
  His love shall enfold thee,
Then sleep, baby, sleep, for thy Saviour is near.

Infant's Christmas Song.

INFANT tongues should ever raise
Sweetest songs on Christmas days;
In a manger, rudely made,
Christ a little child was laid.

Like the shepherds let us haste,
Seek the blessed Christ-child's face;
Saw we never babe so sweet,
Let us worship at His feet.

There's a glory round His head,
Though so low and strange His bed;
Like the magi, let us bring
Unto Him our offering.

Hearts unstained by sin and shame,
Lips that ever praise His name,
Willing feet to walk His ways,
Minds to serve Him all our days.

Song of Praise.

"I will be glad and rejoice in Thee; yea, my songs will I make of Thy name, O Thou Most Highest."

DEAR Lord, my grateful heart would raise
A thankful song of ardent praise,
But all the language that I know
Would fail my joy in Thee to show.

Without Thy love on earth to bless,
This earth were but a wilderness;
No shadowing Rock, no living Bread,
No water from the Fountain-head.

For me, who in Thy love repose,
The desert blossoms as the rose;
By living waters, pure and sweet,
Thou guid'st my weary, wayworn feet,

To rest within the Rock's cool shade,
For heavenward pilgrims kindly made
A refuge and a safe retreat
From angry storms and fervid heat.

When looking back to Calvary
I view what Thou hast done for me;
Thou drain'dst the cup of bitter woe
That mine with joy might overflow.

What can I render, Lord, for this
Thy dying love?—my dear-bought bliss?
I'll praise Thee while my life shall last,
I'll cling to Thee! O hold me fast!

And when Thy shadowy angel, Death,
Shall draw from me life's latest breath,
Then take me where I'll raise a strain
Worthy the Lamb that once was slain.

The Atonement.

At one, my God, with Thee!
What does this mean for me?
    A Friend so near
    I seem to hear
His pleading unto Thee;
    Thy love so deep
    It would not keep
This Friend from agony.

At one, my God, with Thee!
What does this mean for me?
    Pardon and peace,
    And sure release
From sin's dread penalty;
    A perfect dress—
    Christ's righteousness—
In which Thy face to see.

At one, my God, with Thee!
What must this mean for me?
    A narrow way,
    Crossed day by day
With duties set by Thee:
    A willing mind,
    Ever resigned
To what Thou shalt decree.

At one, my God, with Thee!
What must this mean for me?
    An active love,
    By deeds to prove
I share Thy charity:
    Patience and prayer,
    And watchful care
Lest I should part from Thee.

At one, my God, with Thee!
What shall this mean for me?
    After the strife
    The endless life

And crown of victory;
    The promised rest
    In mansions blest,
By Christ prepared for me.

At one, my God, with Thee!
What shall this mean for me?
    A rapture sweet
    When I shall meet
The Friend who rescued me,
    And by His loss,
    And through His cross,
Made me at one with Thee.

Hymn.

Written for the Semi-Centennial Anniversary of St. Paul's Church, Albany, N. Y., Oct. 21, 1877.

ONCE more, O Lord, Thy children come
To praise Thee in the dear church home
Which Thou hast made through years to seem
Like that bright path in Jacob's dream
Where swift-winged angels came and went,
On ministries of love intent.
    For this, O Lord, Thy name we praise,
    And joyful hallelujahs raise,
    And make this earthly temple ring
    With glad hosannas to our King.

For in this place, though all unseen,
Thy messengers of love have been,
Bringing Thy peace to men forgiven,
Returning with their thanks to heaven;

Hymn.

Rejoicing o'er each Christian birth,
Bearing each ransomed soul from earth.

Here Faith hath lent both eyes and wings
To mount and gaze on heavenly things;
Here Hope hath brought her colors rare
And painted pictures wondrous fair,
And Love hath bound, with threefold cord,
Each unto each, all to their Lord.

Here earthly pilgrims, heavenward bound,
Such sweet repose and joy have found
That, though we may not see Thy face,
We know that Thou art in this place,
And by the blessings Thou hast given
Made it the very gate of heaven.

Be with us now as in past days;
Guide us and keep us in Thy ways;
Make every year, as past it flies,
Draw us still nearer to the skies,
That when life's journeys all are done
The heavenly Canaan may be won.

Then in that home Thy name we'll praise,
And joyful hallelujahs raise,
And make Thy heavenly temple ring
With glad hosannas to our King.

Easter Carol.

Awake, awake, and publish
   The joyful news abroad;
The sepulchre is empty,
   And risen is the Lord.
The angels only wait,
   Ere back to heaven they speed,
To tell the weeping mourners
   The Lord is risen indeed.

Awake, awake, and follow,
   The Master goes before
May greet thee in the garden,
   Or meet thee on the shore;
May join thee on life's journey,
   Go with thee to the end,
With words of peace may cheer thee
   And prove thy dearest Friend.

Easter Carol.

Awake, awake, oh, sinner,
    And let the Light shine in
That first upon this morning
    Rose o'er a world of sin.
Wake from thy deadly slumber,
    Thy Saviour bids thee rise
And follow where He leadeth
    Until ye reach the skies.

Awake, awake, and publish
    The joyful news around;
From morning until evening
    Prolong the welcome sound.
The Lord is risen indeed,
    With joy let mortals say
Till He shall come in glory
    At the last Easter day.

My New Neighbor.

WRITTEN ON SEEING A YOUNG AND LOVELY WOMAN INTERRED IN A CITY CHURCH-YARD.

WHAT is my new neighbor like, do you say,
That came to her home next my own to-day?
In truth I know not whether dark or fair;
If golden or brown or raven her hair.

I know those who bore her were sad of mien;
They loved not the task that brought them, I ween,
For the house is narrow and dark and chill,
And they brought her not of their own free will;

But an awful voice had bidden her come,
And she left her dear babes and friends and home

To dwell through all time in the lonesome
    place
Where friends may not enter, nor see her face.

And I know a quiet neighbor she'll be,
For all in that house rest so tranquilly;
Not a sound can come through the fast-closed
    door
Till time shall be over, and death no more.

And thoughts will come of my neighbor to-
    night
As I close my window—put out the light.
Shall I think of the body, in death's embrace,
With closed eyes, sealed lips, and a pale, cold
    face?

Nay! Rather I'll think of the soul's quick
    flight
To its own bright home in mansions of light,
Where the Saviour stands by the open door,
Whom, not having seen, she hath loved before.

The Saviour knoweth all souls that are His,
And welcomes her gladly to realms of bliss;
He bids her rest calmly in Paradise
Till the trumpet shall sound and the dead arise.

She is clothed in beauty celestial now;
The seal of the ransomed set on her brow;
The faithful departed are gathering near,
And voices of loved ones fall sweet on her ear.

So I'll think no more of my neighbor to-night
As out in the church-yard, still and white,
But radiant with joy, in communion sweet
With familiar friends at her Saviour's feet;

And ready to greet, near the open door,
The coming friends she hath loved long before,
Who, entering there through the Saviour's grace,
May behold evermore the dear one's face.

Friends at Sea.

FLOAT lightly, oh, sea, on thy surface to-day,
The ship that is bearing our loved ones away.
Let thy gentle waves lull them as softly to rest
As the mother's sweet song lulls the babe at her breast.
When the storm-god shall come in his terrible might
And lash thy dark waves to a sickening white;
When they, in their agony, leap to the skies,
Then sink in deep waters with moaning and sighs,
May the voice that had power over wild Galilee
Bid the storm-god "be still," whisper "peace" unto thee;
Then praises shall rise from both shores to the Lord
Who ruleth the tempest and calm by His word.

From Geneva to Watkins' Glen.

WITHIN the halls of memory
    Hang pictures of my life;
Some lie in calm and peaceful ways,
    Some 'mid the city's strife;
Some tell of loved departed ones,
    Some of a dear old home,
Others of fair and pleasant lands
    Where I have chanced to roam.

And now again new pictures come
    To claim a little space,
Nor shall those pictures ever fade
    While memory holds her place.
Geneva, on her terraced side,
    Lies bathed in glorious light,
Reflected in the lake's cool depths
    As in a mirror bright.

And then that lake! whose beauty
    The night but half conceals;
No pen or pencil paint the view
    The light of day reveals.
Fair fields and vineyards, mountains
    That tower to kiss the sky,
And lave their feet in waves whose hues
    Are borrowed from on high.

And here and there a village fair
    Lends brightness to the scene,
With Watkins like a diamond
    In crown of emerald green.
Glen Alpha! 'Tis with quickened pulse
    We tread thy narrow ways,
And stop to look with wondrous awe,
    Then follow still the Maze.

In Glen Cathedral's solemn aisle
    We pause with reverent fear;
Shut out from all the world, we feel
    Its Architect is near.

A choir of many waters
    Its ceaseless song doth raise,
A choir that never wearies
    Of its Creator's praise.

Did Senecas of old e'er think
    Here the Great Spirit dwelt?
And as they came within its walls
    His sacred presence felt?
We think it may be so, and yet
    Short time have we for thought:
The things that are have to the Glen
    Our willing footsteps brought.

O'er labyrinthine paths we move
    Through scenes that charm the sight,
Scarce knowing which doth please us most,
    Which give us most delight—
The pictures in the Shadow Gorge,
    The moss upon the wall,
The mirrors in the Glen of Pools,
    The rainbow in the Fall.

With many a lingering look we turn,
    Leaving the Glen behind ;
All left us of its beauties rare
    Are pictures in our mind,
And greater love to God, who made
    Our earthly home so fair,
And gave us eyes of faith to see
    His footprints everywhere.

Easter Thoughts.

"Christ is risen from the dead and become the firstfruits of them that slept. For since by man came death, by man came also the resurrection from the dead."
"My soul fleeth unto the Lord before the morning watch."

WILL Easter ever come to me
    As in the by-gone time
When nought but joyous, happy thoughts
    Came with the early chime?

Thoughts of a Saviour just arisen
    Triumphant from the grave;
Thoughts of the bright hopes newly born
    In those He died to save.

Hopes that had died within the hearts
    Of all that sorrowing band
When the loud, bitter cry was raised,
    And darkness filled the land.

When the bowed head and bleeding side
    Proclaimed death's victory won ;
When the dark grave received their Lord,
    And malice sealed the stone.

But " Christ is risen," the angel said
    To Mary, at the tomb,
And " Christ is risen " revived the hope
    That perished in the gloom.

Last Easter came as bright and fair
    As any since that time ;
The air as pure, the flowers as sweet,
    And just as glad the chime.

But ah! that joyous Easter chime
    Fell on a dying ear ;
The last sound from the outer world
    The dying one would hear,

For angels fair were leading her
    From joys that earth afford,
Through the dark grave and gate of death
    To meet her risen Lord.

Easter Thoughts.

We wonder with what words of cheer
    He met her on the way?
And what the bliss to her revealed
    In Paradise that day?

We know not, nor can heart conceive
    The glories of that place;
We only know that heavenly joys
    Seemed mirrored in her face.

We only know, as gathering clouds
    Obscured that Easter dawn,
So darker shades than e'er before
    Across our path were drawn.

And evermore with Easter morn
    Will thoughts of sadness come,
Yet Christ, the Sun of Righteousness,
    Hath shed around the tomb

Such rays of heavenly light and hope
    To cheer the mourner's heart,
That to shut out all joy with grief
    Would be the heathen's part.

So with a firmer faith we grasp
    The promise He has given,
And hope at the last Easter day
    To meet the loved in heaven.

EASTER EVEN, *April* 15, 1865.

Hymn.

WRITTEN FOR THE MEMORIAL SERVICE OF WILLIAM H. DE WITT, WHO BUILT THE CHURCH OF THE HOLY INNOCENTS, ALBANY, N. Y., IN MEMORY OF FOUR INFANT CHILDREN.

"In Rama was there a voice heard; lamentation, and weeping, and great mourning; Rachel weeping for her children, and would not be comforted because they are not."

THE mothers in Rama sank sweetly to rest,
With dear tender babes in their loving arms pressed;
No warning had they that the tyrant's dread sword
Should make them first martyrs to Jesus, their Lord.

The bright morning dawned o'er the country so fair;
A loud voice of wailing was heard on the air;

The mothers in Rama wept sore for the slain
They never should fold in their fond arms again.

No comfort had they in their dark hour of woe,
Nor knew that Jehovah had ordered it so,
Till lowly they sat at the dear Saviour's feet,
And drew from His teaching this lesson so sweet—

That all who for Him ever suffered and died
Should with Him in glory forever abide,
And they who would enter that home undefiled,
In heart and in spirit must be as a child.

We bless Thee, O Lord, that the infant of days
May glorify Thee, and in death win Thee praise;
We thank Thee, O Lord, that when called to depart
The agèd may be as the child, pure in heart.

That Thy faithful servant, now gone from our
 sight,
In Paradise rests with the children of light;
Oh, grant us Thy grace so to follow Thee here
That we, with Thy servant, in heaven may appear

HOLY INNOCENT'S DAY, 1872.

Hymn.

"Whosoever shall not receive the kingdom of God as a little child, he shall not enter therein."

WE come again, as in past days,
To sing our joyful Christmas lays;
No note of woe should mar the strain
The angels sang o'er Judah's plain.

We come again, as in past days,
To tell the wonders of His ways
Who took from earth an infant band
To praise Him in a fairer land.

To tell how Christ, for whom they died,
Drew little children to His side,
And in His loving arms did press,
And blessed, as only He can bless.

How mourning mothers from that day
"Thy will be done" have learned to say,

And love to think their babes at rest
Upon the gentle Saviour's breast.

And we would breathe a low, sweet strain
As in this place we meet again,
In memory of the faithful friend
Who, loving, served us to the end.

We also bless Thy holy Name,
Who art in every age the same,
That Thou dost gather unto Thee
All souls of child-like purity.

Here in the church he loved so well
Let Thy free Spirit ever dwell,
To cleanse and purify each heart
That in its worship takes a part.

So shall the work that he began
Be blessed unto his fellow-man;
And ransomed souls shall sing Thy praise
With him through everlasting days.

HOLY INNOCENT'S DAY, 1873.

Consecrated Talents.

"Thanks be unto God for His unspeakable gift."

THERE'S a story told of an artisan
   Who fashioned in metal well,
And showed his thanks for the talent God gave
   By making His church a bell.

It rang out with joy to welcome his bride,
   It rang for his children's birth;
It tolled with a sad and solemn sound
   When these treasures were laid in earth.

But a wondrous charm to its tongue was given
   To soothe the woe in his breast;
He knew by the comfort its sweet tones gave
   That in giving he had been blessed.

And he grew to love with a strong, deep love,
   The friend high up in the spire

That seemed to call him from cares of earth
  To holier things, and higher.

He thought of the joy his one gift had brought,
  He thought of the Gift from heaven.
He thought of the thousands of dying men
  To whom new life might be given.

And time and talent and all that he had,
  Every thought and deed and word,
As thanks for His great unspeakable Gift
  He laid at the feet of the Lord.

Then a wondrous charm to his tongue was given
  As he told the message of love,
And he knew by the peace that came to men
  That his work was accepted above.

Anniversary Hymn.

We enter, Lord, with gladness
  Thy sacred courts to-day;
We banish thoughts of sadness,
  And raise a thankful lay,
With cheerful hearts and voices
  We raise the joyful strain,
And pray that Thou wilt bless us
  Until we meet again.

In mercy Thou hast brought us
  This bright, glad day to see,
And by Thy Spirit taught us
  How we may live for Thee.
With cheerful hearts and voices
  We raise the joyful strain,
And pray that Thou wilt bless us
  Until we meet again.

Anniversary Hymn.

In kindness Thou hast taken
   Some loved ones from our eyes,
But only to awaken
   With Thee in Paradise.
With cheerful hearts and voices
   We raise the joyful strain,
And pray that Thou wilt bless us
   Until we meet again.

And when on earth forever
   These tongues shall silent be,
Then take us where we never
   Shall cease from praising Thee.
With cheerful hearts and voices
   We raise the parting strain,
And pray that Thou wilt keep us
   Until we meet again.

Easter Memories.

BRIGHT Easter Morn! sad memories
   Come thronging with thy light.
Sad memories of sad, sad days,
   And a far sadder night
When in the shadow of the grave
   Our well-beloved lay,
And wrestled with the angel Death
   Until the break of day.

Wrestled until the blessing came
   Of everlasting peace,
And perfect rest from care and pain
   'Mid joys that never cease.
Rest with the saints in Paradise,
   Rest with the loved ones gone,
Rest with her Saviour, till shall break
   The last great Easter morn.

Easter Memories.

Glad Easter bells! sad memories
   Are with your notes combined;
One Easter morn thy merry tunes
   Came floating on the wind,
Came floating through the casement
   Unto the dying ear
Of one who never more on earth
   Sweet melodies should hear,

For ere thy chimes had ceased to ring
   The joyous Easter in,
Her spirit left its home of clay,
   Of weakness, pain, and sin,
And cheered by heavenly music
   From bright angelic bands,
She sought beyond the gates of death
   "A house not made with hands."

Sweet Easter flowers! sad memories
   Are with thy beauties blent,
For flowers that through the hallowed fane
   Their fragrant odors sent,

Were brought to cheer the saddened home,
    Where lay our sainted dead,
And speak to us of hope in death,
    When hope in life had fled.

To speak, with sweetly silent voice,
    The resurrection power
Of Him who from the earth's dark tomb
    Had raised each beauteous flower.
Who, victor over Death and Hell
    And o'er the insatiate grave,
Had risen, the firstfruits from the dead,
    The Life, with power to save.

Dear Easter hopes! sad memories
    Shall gladden in thy light
As surely as the coming day
    Dispels the shades of night.
As surely as the Light that broke
    Upon the world that day
Brought life to view, and took from death
    The bitterness away.

Then in this light will we rejoice,
    And sorrow not as those
Around whose friends, untinged with hope,
    Death's darkest shadows close.
Ring out, ye bells, your gladdest lay!
    Still breathe of hope, ye flowers!
The voice that to her heart spake peace,
    Shall whisper "peace" to ours.

The Angel at the Sepulchre.

WHENEVER we think or read of the Angel at the Sepulchre an ideal always comes to our mind; an ideal so beautiful that it is ever welcome to the place it has assumed.*
We saw it first when the artist was giving the final touches to this grand creation of his genius, and as we stood in awe before its majestic purity, could not but hope he might long remain with us who could so embody the spirit of beauty in "the beauty of holiness." We saw it last in the "City of the Dead," where surrounding loveliness enhanced every grace. Encircled by living green; standing in bold relief against a background of deepest blue, with just one ray of golden

---

* A monument, by Palmer, in the Albany Rural Cemetery, to the memory of Mrs. Robert Lenox Banks.

light from the western sky touching the face, it was something one could not easily forget. It seemed not like cold marble, but like a living watcher over the sleeping dead, only waiting until the resurrection morn to speak words of joy, and lead them to their risen and ascended Lord.

Why come ye to this lower world,
    Bright angel from above?
Why leave the realms of glorious light,
    Of purest joy and love,
To linger in the gloomy dawn
    Beside an earthly tomb
Whose open door, with broken seal,
    Shows but an empty room?

No minister of wrath art thou,
    To grasp the avenging sword;
Not thine to execute on earth
    The terrors of the Lord.
Though majesty doth sit serene
    Upon thy lofty brow,

Too near Love's throne thy place hath been
  To lose Love's image now.

Why tarry then? and who are they
  The sun's first rays reveal?
They surely can not roll the stone,
  They dare not break Rome's seal!
They pause in doubt—then hasten on
  Toward the sacred place;
In mute surprise they gaze around,
  Then look upon thy face.

And this is why thou lingerest?
  Thou hast somewhat to tell
To these sad women at the tomb!
  Oh, it shall please them well,
For never yet bore messenger
  Such words of holy cheer!
"The Lord is risen, go seek Him hence,
  Thou canst not find Him here."

The Lord is risen! that glorious strain
  Shall never die away

Till thou shalt come with that dear One
   At the last Easter day,
To bid the dead in Him arise
   And with the quick ascend,
That they who sought an unseen Lord
   May find a present Friend.

Children's Te Deum.

WE praise Thee, O God;
   Thy children shall sing
With all things on earth
   That worship their King,
While angels and cherubs
   And seraphs do cry,
And Holy, thrice Holy,
   Resound through the sky.

Prophets and martyrs,
   Apostles praise Thee;
The Church in all places
   Wherever it be
Doth own Thee as Father,
   Thy Son ever bless,
And both, with the Spirit
   One God doth confess.

Children's Te Deum.

Thou Christ, as the King
   Of glory we own,
Who humbly to earth
   Came down from Thy throne
To win for believers,
   Through death's sharpest pain,
A home everlasting
   In glory again.

Save, Lord, Thy people,
   Thine heritage bless;
Govern and keep us
   From sin and distress.
Lord Jesus, have mercy;
   We trust in Thy name,
Have mercy upon us,
   And save us from shame.

Christmas Carols.

I.

O BLESSED Lord Jesus, we sing to Thy praise
The sweetest glad songs that our voices can raise.
With joy do we hasten Thy coming to greet,
And hailing Thee Saviour, bend low at Thy feet.

CHORUS.

The angels are singing Thy praise through the sky,
Earth's glad voices ringing shall join theirs on high;
Deep unto deep calleth, thanksgiving to raise,
And mountains and valleys break forth into praise.

O blessed Lord Jesus, we heed not that Thou
Hast come to the earth in humility now;

We know that the prophets and sages of old
No splendor or pomp at Thy coming foretold.

O blessed Lord Jesus, Thy coming to earth
Has given earth's children a glorious birth ;
Now God is our Father, our Brother Thou art,
Make quickly Thy home in each fond waiting
heart.

O blessed Lord Jesus, bright star of our night,
Make glad all the nations that walk in Thy
light.
Shine on in Thy brightness, the heathen to
bless,
Till all tongues united Thy name shall confess.

II.

Down through the clouds in the silent night,
Far from their homes in glorious light,
Came fair angels to sing o'er the earth
The joyful news of the Saviour's birth.

Chorus.

And the heavens rang
With the song they sang,
There is peace on the earth, good-will to man,
And glory to God in the highest.

The listening shepherds heard the sound,
And saw the wonderful light around,
And heard the voice of an angel say,
"There are glad tidings for you to-day."

They came in haste to the lowly place,
And looked with joy on the Christ-child's face;
No offerings rare had they to bring,
But they worshipped Him as Lord and King.

The magi wise, in the east afar,
Saw the light that seemed a guiding star,
And following, came where its radiance shed
A holy light round an infant's head.

The gifts they brought were costly and rare,
Such gifts as for great ones only are,
But they laid them at the infant's feet,
And deemed that for Him such gifts were
 meet.

Oh, rich and wise, bring your gifts to-day,
And join with earth's poor ones to swell the
 lay
That first was heard on that Christmas night,
When angels came from the realms of light
   And the heavens rang
   With the song they sang,
There is peace on earth, good-will to man,
 And glory to God in the highest.

III.

Ring out, ring out, O Christmas bells!
A tale of joy your music tells;
A Saviour King was born to-day
To rule the hearts of men for aye.

Chorus.

> For this we join to swell the strain
> The angels sang o'er Judah's plain;
> Glory to God, good-will to men
> Shall rise and fill the heavens again.

O Lord of lords and King of kings,
Sweet peace and joy Thy presence brings;
We know the Father loved us well
To rescue thus our souls from hell.

But who can measure all the love
That brought Thee from Thy throne above,

With us to live, for us to die,
That we might dwell with Thee on high.

Dear Saviour, elder Brother, Friend,
Abide with us till life shall end;
And then, when death shall set us free,
Within the kingdom won by Thee,

Earth's ransomed ones shall swell the strain
All worthy is the Lamb once slain,
" Honor and glory to receive
From all created things that breathe."

Pilate's Question.

WHAT shall I do with Jesus, called the Christ?
This lone, strange man! So sad and yet so calm;
So awful in His silent majesty
I fear the power He spake of may be His
To crush me if I do this evil deed.
For well I know 'tis evil. Fault there's none.
His innocence doth so envelope Him,
I could not think Him guilty if I would.
And yet methinks if He hath any power
'Twere never better used than now to hurl
Defiance at these envious, hateful Jews,
And wreak His vengeance on the coward crew
That e'en desert Him in His direst need.
I fain would save Him, for my heart is stirred
To pity it hath never known before.
Pity and Fear! Strange feelings these for Pilate!
Shall I hold to them, and make my nobler

Conquer my baser self? Or shall I make
Myself a slave to serve these angry dogs
That cry for blood, and will not be appeased
Though blood were offered, if it be not His,
And grudge me if they be not satisfied?

Yet why should I—a Roman—lose one chance
For place or power to succor one so friend-
    less?
Deserted, save by a few weak women;
One voice alone upraised to plead for Him,
And that the voice of one who may lose most
If I am merciful. From the vast throng
That followed where He went, and heard the
    words
That fell as graciously upon their ears
As falls the evening dew on sun-scorched
    flowers,
Comes not one sound to help me choose the
    right,
Or strengthen good resolves. His blood—
    they cry—
Be on us and our children. Let it be.

I'll wash my hands to prove my innocence;
Then yield Him to them.

What shall I do with Jesus? Ever now
Between me and the things I look upon
Comes a clear vision of that pale, worn face,
With its last look of awful agony
That will not be put out in darkest night.
When sleep comes not, then is the vision there;
And when sleep comes, then comes that face
    in dreams.
When morning dawns and with its veil of
    light
Shuts out the stars, it shuts not out from me
The dazzling brightness of those searching
    eyes.
The burning glances of a thousand midday
    suns
Upon my naked sight were not so hard to bear.
I could curse the nation that drove me on
To do the deed, conscience, seared though it
    was,
Still told me I should bitterly repent.

Oh, would that I had known that day the
    power
An outraged conscience doth possess to goad
The mind to madness—take all joy from life.
Banished, deserted, homeless, powerless,
Haunted forever by that face, and thoughts
Of that one deed that make me ever feel
That it were better I had not been born,
What can life hold for such a wretch as I?
And death? I dare not look upon it,
For ere I left the Syrian shore I heard
Christ's followers proclaim a risen Lord,
And reason well of judgment yet to come.
Can it be that in that dreaded future
Our places shall be changed? I the culprit?
He the Judge? If I trembled even then
Before His gaze, where, where shall I hide me
If these things be true? And that they are
I am as sure as of His innocence.
Oh, miserable man! Comfortless; hopeless;
Trembling I ask, "What will He do with
    me?"

What shall I do with Jesus? For himself
Must each one ask and answer Pilate's question.
For the dear Lord still waiteth patiently,
With pleading face, and tender, wistful look,
For words that put Him to an open shame
Or hold Him in the closest bonds of love.
O soul immortal! What shall be thy choice?
To send Him sad and sorrowing from thee now,
Or make of Him thy Friend, that in that day
When thou shalt stand before the Judgment-seat
Thou mayest not fear what He will do with thee.

Two Voices.

SUGGESTED by a picture by the celebrated French painter, Horace Vernet, of the "Angel of Death bearing off a young girl." A youth at her side has hidden his face, that he may not see the approach of the "King of Terrors," who comes to the girl, not as the grinning, ghastly skeleton we so often see represented, but as an angelic messenger, with a form dark and mysterious, it is true, but a face, when closely inspected, of celestial beauty, and a touch too gentle to disturb the impress of her form on the couch from which he is raising her, while the youth seems unconscious of his presence.

I.

Oh, horrid, grim, and ghastly death!
Thou comest with thy chilling breath
To wither all the flowers of hope
    That in my pathway lie.

The fairest maid these eyes have seen
Was mine to woo and win, I ween;
'Twas only on life's downward slope
    I thought that she might die.

By pleasant paths, o'er fragrant flowers,
I hoped to lead my love to bowers
And shady nooks of living green,
    Where zephyrs wander free.
Love's rosy light I thought would last,
But thou hast come to overcast
Its glowing morn, and stand between
    My cherished one and me.

I can not see thee grasp her hand
And lead her to the unknown land
Through dismal shades, where phantoms grim
    May freeze her soul with fright.
O Reason! thy poor, flickering ray
Lures but to darken sorrow's day,
For Death is king where faith is dim,
    And thine the only light.

II.

My loving, patient watcher sleeps;
The long, sad vigil that he keeps
Beside my couch has wearied him
    E'en to forgetfulness.
Dear Father, in Thy love impart
Some solace to his breaking heart;
The cup Thou fillest to the brim
    With anguish, do Thou bless.

Give him the faith Thou givest to me—
The faith beyond this world to see
A glorious realm where Thou art King,
    Nor sin, nor death shall reign.
I feel the messenger is near
That parts me from my loved one here;
But thou, O Death, hast lost thy sting,
    Christ's dead shall live again.

So gently dost thou draw me hence,
So softly steal my soul from sense
And bear me on to Paradise
    To meet my Saviour dear,

Though dim and shadowy thou art,
No terror doth thy form impart;
There is a look within thine eyes
    Forbids all thought of fear.

It may be I shall pass to light
Through shadows darker than the night,
But since my Lord hath been that way
    I will not dread the tomb:
I know that I can trust His power
Most fully in the darkest hour;
His promise is—to be my stay
    Until I leave the gloom.

www.ingramcontent.com/pod-product-compliance
Lightning Source LLC
Chambersburg PA
CBHW020314090426
42735CB00009B/1344